a pocketful
RHYME
Imagination for a new generation

2006 Poetry Competition for 7-11 year-olds

YoungWriters

South Wales Vol I
Edited by Donna Samworth

 Young**Writers**

First published in Great Britain in 2006 by:
Young Writers
Remus House
Coltsfoot Drive
Peterborough
PE2 9JX
Telephone: 01733 890066
Website: www.youngwriters.co.uk

SB ISBN 1 84602 475 7

Foreword

Young Writers was established in 1991 and has been passionately devoted to the promotion of reading and writing in children and young adults ever since. The quest continues today. Young Writers remains as committed to the nurturing of poetic and literary talent as ever.

This year's Young Writers competition has proven as vibrant and dynamic as ever and we are delighted to present a showcase of the best poetry from across the UK and in some cases overseas. Each poem has been selected from a wealth of *A Pocketful Of Rhyme* entries before ultimately being published in this, our fourteenth primary school poetry series.

Once again, we have been supremely impressed by the overall quality of the entries we have received. The imagination, energy and creativity which has gone into each young writer's entry made choosing the poems a challenging and often difficult but ultimately hugely rewarding task - the general high standard of the work submitted ensured this opportunity to bring their poetry to a larger appreciative audience.

We sincerely hope you are pleased with this final collection and that you will enjoy *A Pocketful Of Rhyme South Wales Vol I* for many years to come.

Contents

Terrace Road Primary School, Swansea

Liam Pitson (9)	33
Samuel Wyatt (9)	34
Ben Taylor (9)	35
Charlotte Adams (9)	36
Jodi Sarsero (10)	37
Joshua Sullivan (9)	38
Joseph Freeman (9)	39
Rebekah Ellis (9)	40
Sakariya Abdi (9)	41
Rhys Thomas (10)	42
Sam Davies (10)	43
Luke Harris (9)	44

Tredegarville CW Primary School, Cardiff

Belal Ahmad (11)	45
Levi Charles (9)	46
Rachel Cazenave-Smith (10)	47
Danielle Hall (10)	48
Breeze Thompson (10)	49
Lauren Trickett (10)	50
Mica Schiazza (11)	51
Zahra Chowdhury (8)	52
Jacob Charles (8)	53
Michaela Williams (8)	54
Shannon Manfield (Age?)	55
Joshua Trickett (8)	56
Corey Stephens (7)	57
Samantha Carter (8)	58
Kieran Fitzpatrick (8)	59
Rachael Woodrow (11)	60
Talal Hesham Ghrairi (11)	61
Kieren Pash (11)	62
Daniel Kilford (10)	63
Atlanta Hewings (10)	64
Isaac Kahar (11)	65
Chelsea Copp (11)	66
Shanice Burnett (11)	67
Natasha Wilkinson (10)	68

Trellech Primary School, Monmouth

Joe Paley (11)	69
Abbie Ellicott (11)	70
Tom Kedward (11)	71
Bethan Gorvett (11)	72
Lakota Gunter (10)	73
Sean McMahon (10)	74
Ben Hyde (11)	75
Gabrielle Jones (11)	76
Emily Kedward (10)	77
Sam Land (10)	78
Andrew Morgan (10)	79
Nicola Bowen (11)	80
Liam Musselbrook (11)	81
Harry King (11)	82
Zoe Horsfield (10)	83
Tom Kelly (10)	84
Bethan King (8)	85
Stephanie Warner (9)	86
Lianne Edwards (9)	87
Edward Land (8) & Robert Bowen (8)	88
Matthew Casson (9)	89
Morgan Paley (9)	90
Daniel Musselbrook (9)	91
Christopher Widdicks (9)	92
Briony Waycott (9)	93
Bethany Powell (8)	94
Kirsten Jeffs (7)	95
Thomas Bristow (8)	96
Bradd Morgan-Bowen (9)	97
Emily Pardington (8)	98
Emily Pettitt (8)	99
Alice Pettitt (8)	100
Joshua Rodgers (8)	101
Kitty Jones (8)	102
George Burnett (7)	103

Tutshill CE Primary School, Chepstow

Hannah Pockett (10)	104
Sophie Piccirilli (9)	105
Jack Fear (9)	106

Ysgol Cynlais, Swansea

Ystruth School, Abertillery

The Poems

In The Workhouse

I was sent to the workhouse when I was nine,
It seems as if I've been here a very long time,
When I got here the gates were so big,
The meals we ate were fit for a pig!

When we arrived families were split up,
We didn't have possessions, not even a cup,
Horrible clothes they made us wear,
If we got ill no one would care!

Christmas Day was just the same,
Not a present, not a game,
The work we do goes on and on,
You could hear someone say, 'I want my mom.'

Where's my mum? Where's my dad?
It feels as if my mind's gone mad,
I pricked my finger then it bled,
'I think I'm going to die,' I said.

Sadie Robertson & Paige Davies (10)
Our Lady & St Michael's RC Primary School, Abergavenny

Love Is . . .

Love is a deep, deep red like bursting blood.
It's when you cherish someone and never leave their heart.
It is elegant music.
Love looks like hearts and Cupid floating through the air.
It smells like freshly picked strawberries with sugar sprinkled all over.
Love is a tingly feeling like a shot of electricity.
Love is a feeling like sailing on a quilt of redness.
Love comes to you when you find someone you desire.

Lara Boyd (9)
Our Lady & St Michael's RC Primary School, Abergavenny

Excitement Is . . .

Excitement is blue like the sky dashing around the clouds.
Excitement is the beautiful air going in your face.
Excitement is singing voices echoing.
Excitement is sweets and candy drifting through the air.
Excitement is a hot plate with chips and nuggets.
It looks like sunlight in the sky, shining all around us.
It feels like playing on the hopscotch in the playground.
Excitement is when you get a dog and teach him to come
And you play with him.

Joshua Badham (10)
Our Lady & St Michael's RC Primary School, Abergavenny

Embarrassment Is . . .

Embarrassment slithers up when no one is looking,
His taste is bitter and unpleasant.
His appearance is not much better,
He's lumpy and bumpy and looks like he's swelling.
The smell is like rotting cheese left in the cupboard.
His colour is bright red so when his creeping up on you,
You'll have to share his colour too.
He sounds like glass shattering on the floor,
Once embarrassment has come happiness is no more!

Yasmina Price (9)
Our Lady & St Michael's RC Primary School, Abergavenny

Happiness Is . . .

Happiness is a frog jumping up and down on the pond,
Happiness is sweets and chocolate in your mouth,
Happiness is your best friends who care for you,
It is the blue sky which is moving around the world.
Happiness is love.

Nichelle Punzal (9)
Our Lady & St Michael's RC Primary School, Abergavenny

Sadness . . .

Sadness is a tear dropping from your eye.
Sadness is the colour of darkness.
Sadness is a heart split into half.
Sadness is a smile that's gone.
Sadness tastes like sprouts that are rotten.
Sadness is someone who has died in your family.
Sadness smells like toast that's been burnt.
Sadness is a boy that's been bullied.
Sadness is paper that's been ripped.
Sadness is a game that you lose.

Jose Doruelo (9)
Our Lady & St Michael's RC Primary School, Abergavenny

Fear Is . . .

Fear is black stormy clouds.
It tastes like broccoli.
Fear is a quiet and dark road.
It is the sound of stamping footsteps.
Fear feels like being squeezed.
It's so quiet that you can hear your heartbeats.
Fear is a blueberry being squashed.
It is the sound of lightning.
Fear is being on your own.

Agatha Fayette (9)
Our Lady & St Michael's RC Primary School, Abergavenny

Laughter

Laughter is yellow like stars twinkling in the clear night sky.
Laughter sounds like hip hop music flowing through the air.
Laughter is teasing people to make it seem funny.
Laughter is a joke that I laugh about.
Laughter makes you feel happy and joyful.
Laughter smells like breath and fresh air.

Garryn West (11)
Our Lady & St Michael's RC Primary School, Abergavenny

Happiness

Happiness reminds me of the rich green and golds of the valley,
With shadows quivering out into the tranquil countryside.
Happiness is like a multicoloured star glistening in the moonlit sky.
Happiness smells like a freshly cooked English breakfast
On an early Sunday morn, with the blackbirds chirping merrily.
Happiness tastes like chocolate sizzling away in your mouth,
All slithering down your chin.
Happiness sounds like laughter chuckling in the background.

Caitlin Thomas (10)
Our Lady & St Michael's RC Primary School, Abergavenny

Sadness

Sadness is a darkened blue
Like the night sky at dusk.
Sadness tastes terrible and dry
Like being right in the middle of a desert
Without any food or water.
Sadness feels cold and lonely
Like no one has a care in the world.
Sadness smells like an old, rotted, dead body
Right in front of you.
Sadness sounds like someone wailing and crying
And it seems like it will never stop.

Thomas Cozens (10)
Our Lady & St Michael's RC Primary School, Abergavenny

Hunger

Hunger tastes like hot ash in your throat
burning your insides out.

Hunger sounds like voices in your head
telling you your time is up.

Hunger feels like hot ash and dust
covered stones, in a hot desert.

Hunger looks like a sandstorm, blinding
your eyes and ripping you apart.

Hunger reminds you of roast chicken
and toast.

Hunger is the colour of jet-black and
misty-brown and grey.

Hunger smells like a foul rotten black pit.

Torin Hillman (11)
Our Lady & St Michael's RC Primary School, Abergavenny

Laughter

Laughter is scarlet like a bouncing ball
going up and down glimmering like the sea.

Laughter smells like chocolate and
marshmallows melting on a campfire.

Laughter feels like a fuzzy feeling inside you
like hot chocolate running down your throat.

Laughter looks like a funny face
winking at you.

Laughter reminds me of having fun
with all of my mates on a day trip out.

Laughter sounds like when one of your friends
cracks a joke and you can't stop laughing.

Laughter tastes like a barbecue with burgers
and hot dogs cooking in the summer.

Katie Palmer (10)
Our Lady & St Michael's RC Primary School, Abergavenny

Hunger

Hunger is turquoise because blue and green are like
someone starving.
Hunger looks like a whirlwind swirling around everywhere.

Hunger tastes of nothing,
Hunger sounds like a person wailing in the stomach.
Hunger feels like sand running through my fingers.

Hunger reminds me of a rumbly stomach with the hunger for food.
Hunger smells like a starving scent.

Ned Bramley (10)
Our Lady & St Michael's RC Primary School, Abergavenny

Fear

Fear is black like the fur of a werewolf, leaping and bounding
towards you.
Fear smells like rotting corpses spread out before you.
Fear tastes like rotten eggs that fill you with horror the moment
you eat them.
Fear reminds you of the most horrible thing that ever happened to you.
Fear sounds like someone being murdered slowly and painfully,
Screaming out with pain.

Sam Hooton (10)
Our Lady & St Michael's RC Primary School, Abergavenny

Cruelty

Cruelty is burgundy like a dog being kicked onto the street
By a hard-hearted person.
Cruelty sounds like a baby crying and screaming, not being cared for.
Cruelty smells like smoke chasing you into a corner.
Cruelty looks like hounds ripping foxes apart.
Cruelty reminds me of torture and bad news.
Cruelty feels like getting hurt by other people as they pick on you.

Stacey Griffiths (11)
Our Lady & St Michael's RC Primary School, Abergavenny

Hate

Hate is black like a bitter cold day in the heart of winter.
Hate feels like a million knives stabbing you endlessly.
Hate tastes vile, like a deadly acid burning your throat.
Hate smells like gone off cheese rotting at the back of a cupboard.
Hate reminds me of someone who murders.
Hate sounds like an evil animal snarling, ready for the kill.

Megan Davey (10)
Our Lady & St Michael's RC Primary School, Abergavenny

Happiness

Happiness smells like the most amazing perfume you've ever smelt.
Happiness is rich red like no colour you've ever seen.
Happiness sounds like children happily playing all day in a
                                              paddling pool.
Happiness tastes like the milkiest chocolate you've ever tasted.
Happiness looks like a nice sunny day where everybody is joyful.

Jay Griffiths (10)
Our Lady & St Michael's RC Primary School, Abergavenny

Loneliness Is . . .

Loneliness is a cold sea.
Loneliness is like being a ghost.
Loneliness is when nobody notices you, or cares for you.
Cold sea goes to your heart and no one's there.
Loneliness is freezing cold like ice.
Loneliness is cold blood going through you.
It reminds me of mud, horrible mud laughing at you.
No one looks at you or talks to you.
Loneliness is like cold rice.
Loneliness is coldness from the freezer.
Loneliness is the taste of gone off chicken.
It's not nice being lonely.

Bethan Jones (10)
Our Lady & St Michael's RC Primary School, Abergavenny

Monkey Mania

Monkey, monkey scratching a flea,
Monkey, monkey watch out for that tree.
Monkey, monkey flying through the air,
Monkey, monkey into a lion's lair.

Monkey, monkey I love you,
Monkey, monkey chew, chew, chew.

Monkey, monkey an ape, an ape,
Monkey, monkey escape, escape.
Monkey, monkey don't get eaten,
Monkey, monkey don't get beaten.

Monkey, monkey I love you,
Monkey, monkey chew, chew, chew.

Jordan Harman (11)
Pentwynmawr Primary School, Newbridge

My Brother And I

My brother and I are completely different,
He's more like a monkey swinging through the trees,
I'm more like a butterfly in all shapes and colours,
He likes cars and games,
As I like flowers and books,
His favourite colour is blue,
I like lilac and pink,
But there are a few things that we do like the same and they are,
Playing together,
Swimming
And we're always happy,
So OK we're not completely different.

Alice Preece (10)
Pentwynmawr Primary School, Newbridge

When I Grow Up

When I grow up I'd like to be an athlete running for that gold medal,
I'd feel like I've won the world and it's all to myself,
I'd see gold sparkles sparkling everywhere,
I would taste the sweet sense of success,
I would smell roses falling all around me,
It would make me so happy I would want to win again,
I would hear the crowd cheering and clapping for me,
It would have been the happiest day of my life standing
On that stage looking at the crowd.

Angharad Lloyd (9)
Pentwynmawr Primary School, Newbridge

Haunted House

I saw this haunted house,
The doors squeak like a mouse,
And when I went inside,
I felt like going to hide.
I was scared of something,
Like a monster jumping out,
And when I went upstairs
I thought I'd seen a bear.
Then when I ran back down,
I saw a scruffy crown,
I ran to my right,
But nothing was in sight.
Then I ran to the door,
Scared and frightened then I saw,
A gigantic shadow heading this way,
So I turned around and ran away,
Out the door and down the steps,
With my little bag named Tex.

Corey Lewis (11)
Pentwynmawr Primary School, Newbridge

Things I Love

Mouth-watering vinegar sprinkled on chips,
When my fingers are cold, warm woolly mitts,
Fairies magic and a dragon with a fierce look,
On a hot day dipping my feet into a freezing cold pool,
Maybe school!
Music in my room,
I play it loud, *boom, boom, boom,*
I love all kinds of dogs,
Almost every animal, even slimy frogs,
Life is very precious and dear to me,
But most of all I love my family!

Nyree Dunn (10)
Pentwynmawr Primary School, Newbridge

Animals

Horses make noises such as *clip-clop,*
Hares jump far in only one hop,
Alligators snap at things they don't like,
I would laugh if a seal could ride a bike,
Puppies are weird when they pounce,
So are kittens when they bounce,
A monkey's chatter is like a baboon's natter,
Mice are quiet when they creep,
Toads jump high when they leap,
Now a fox comes rushing past,
He finds his prey at last,
Horses make noises such as *clip-clop,*
Hares jump far in only one hop.

Ceri Lloyd (10)
Pentwynmawr Primary School, Newbridge

Rugby

Pass, pass get it to the left,
Pass, pass get it to the right,
Hit the tackles as hard as you can,
Get support quick as you can.

Pass, pass get it to the right,
Pass, pass get it to the left,
Flick it out of a scrum,
Let the fly-half have some fun.

Pass, pass get it to the left,
Pass, pass get it to the right,
Hand them off,
Hit them low,
Pildrive through them and go!

Pass, pass get it to the right,
Pass, pass get it to the left,
Go for drop kick from far out,
Punt it over for a chase.

Pass, pass get it to the left,
Pass, pass get it to the right,
I don't want to make it complicated, so,
Just pass it!

Rory Barrett (10)
Pentwynmawr Primary School, Newbridge

Sea Life

While fishing in the deep blue sea,
Something exciting sat on my knee,
A talking fish span with glee,
His scales so shiny,
His fins so small,
But then he span back into the deep blue sea.

While fishing in the deep blue sea,
Something exciting sat on my knee,
A waddling sea horse waddled with me,
His tail so curly,
His fins so big,
But then this sea horse waddled back into the deep blue sea.

While fishing in the deep blue sea,
Something exciting sat on my knee,
A clipper's crab clipped my knee,
His clippers so sharp,
His legs so small,
But then this crab clipped back into the deep blue sea.

Ashleigh Bowles (10)
Pentwynmawr Primary School, Newbridge

The Haunted Mansion

In the haunted mansion
The walls are as dusty as a duster,
The rooms are full of clutter,
The floorboards creak
While you sleep,
The mice squeak,
There are no lights,
There is a rat that bites,
You will have a shock,
The big birds flock,
The doors slam
With a bang.

Look in the mirror, what's behind?
You know what you see,
You say to yourself, *it couldn't be.*
It gets closer,
The heart gets faster,
Look in the mirror again,
Feel the pain,
It is no longer there,
All you do is stare,
You think to yourself, *what could it be?*
There was definitely something behind me.
Look again,
There is something there,
It comes behind you,
Feel the pain,
Then he disappears again.

Jake Roberts (10)
Pentwynmawr Primary School, Newbridge

My Favourite Place

My favourite place is warm,
My favourite place feels so soft,
My favourite place is delightful,
My favourite place is safe,
My favourite place is delicious,
My favourite place is fun,
My favourite place is nice,
My favourite place is never-ending,
My favourite place is with you.

Gabriella Wysom (11)
Pentwynmawr Primary School, Newbridge

RBS 6 Nations

The 6 Nations is a tournament,
Rugby is exciting,
Rugby is passionate,
I can see everyone wearing their team's tops
And raising their flags,
I can hear people chanting, 'Wales,' 'England,' 'France,'
I can see so much red it's like the world is red,
I hope the reigning champs Wales will win again.

Jacob Allen (11)
Pentwynmawr Primary School, Newbridge

The Haunted House

Hear the creaks,
Hear the cries,
Hear the shouts,
Hear the sighs,
When you enter the house today,
Just be careful what you say.

See the dark and gloomy lake,
Go in the house and have a shake.
Careful of the creepy cries,
The clever work, the scary disguise,
Hear the scary music play,
At the wonderful holiday,
Come and play,
What do you say?
Have a fright,
Wanna bite?
Come and see the rainforest,
Then you can meet the vampire Boris,
I agree and go ahead,
Then I get trapped on the bed,
Boris comes flying with a *wheee,*
Then he sucks the blood out of me.

Joely Stredwick (11)
Pentwynmawr Primary School, Newbridge

Brothers

My brother likes chocolate, he likes ice cream too and jelly,
After that he gets a big belly,
He sneaks sweets up in his room,
You smell them in the morning,
You can hear him munching in the night
And gulping Coca-Cola,
Then you hear him being sick,
Mum lets him off school the next day,
Mum says he looks pale but he's only gone
And put white eye shadow on his face,
Brothers, hey, what can we do with them?

Shelby Ann Williams (10)
Pentwynmawr Primary School, Newbridge

Monkey Man

Monkey man, monkey man swinging through the trees,
Monkey man, monkey man as dirty as can be,
Monkey man, monkey man smells like me,
Monkey man, monkey man as big as can be,
Monkey man, monkey man reminds me of King Kong,
Monkey man, monkey man chases after me,
All he wants to do is the limbo with me,
Monkey man, monkey man loses against me,
Monkey man, monkey man goes on a tantrum and kills everything
                                                    he sees,

Monkey man, monkey man calm down please,
Monkey man, monkey man tries to kill me,
Monkey man calms down when I'm out of sight,
Monkey man my friend forever, is that all right?

Lewes Jenkins (9)
Pentwynmawr Primary School, Newbridge

Desert Dance

Desert, desert,
Dancing in the desert.
Like a lizard lifting his feet.
Like a side-winder twisting and turning.
Wobbling like a camel's hump.
Waving my arms like a beetle burrowing,
Elegant as an ostrich.
Bells on our ankles like sheep and goats
Let's all dance
In the desert.

Liam Pitson (9)
Terrace Road Primary School, Swansea

Sahara

Where is there sand hills like waves of the sea?
Where is there sand glowing like red-hot sparks.
Where is there heat like a burning flame,
Sahara, Sahara, Sahara.

The heat is getting too much in the fiery pit,
The heat is too much to bear.
The heat is still increasing,
I need water quickly or I will perish.

At last water, water, water,
Dip my face in precious water.
I need to drink gallons by the minute,
Now I have found the lights of Mecca
Shining in the darkness.
I know I am not lost now
As I hear the sound of people I feel safe.

Samuel Wyatt (9)
Terrace Road Primary School, Swansea

Desert
How Do We Survive

Desert, desert, desert
Hot and dry desert
No water, no food, how do we survive?
Camels and people walking their way.
Desert, desert,
How do we survive?
It's a place of death,
How do we survive?
No shop, no houses.
I feel hot, I feel dry,
How do we survive?
Sand, sand, sand
That's all that's there
Desert, desert, desert
Horrifying desert,
Scorching desert.
No shade, lots of blaze,
Sand, sand, sand
Sand, sand, sand.
It's like walking on fire,
All I desire is some water.

Ben Taylor (9)
Terrace Road Primary School, Swansea

The Sahara Desert

The desert, the desert, the Sahara,
The desert, the desert, where life is harder.

With vast sand dunes
That tower so high
And stretch all the way to the horizon sky.

Camels are the only transport
Which travels the desert, from port to port.

Meeting a stranger could help you survive,
And find an oasis to keep you alive!

The desert, the desert, try as you might,
The desert, the desert, your life is a fight.

Charlotte Adams (9)
Terrace Road Primary School, Swansea

Sand

Oceans of sand hills and waves
Help from strangers along the way.
150° all day long
You can hardly bear the sun.
Water, water, I need water
Dragging myself through the yellow sand.
I can barely stand.
Life, life!
I need the water of life.

Jodi Sarsero (10)
Terrace Road Primary School, Swansea

Sahara Desert

There is sand in the desert,
Lots and lots of sand in the desert.
Desert is a place of death, death, death.
Scorching desert, how do we survive?
How do we survive?
If I was a house plant, I would die in the desert,
Desert, desert.

Desert, how do we survive?
Desert is death, death, death.
Desert how do we survive?
Desert is death, death, death.

Camels have a hump, hump, hump,
Which stores fat, fat, fat.

Desert how do we survive?
Desert is death, death, death.
Desert, how do we survive?
Desert is death, death, death.

Camels can carry 1000kg,
1000kg, 1000kgs.

Joshua Sullivan (9)
Terrace Road Primary School, Swansea

Desert Song

Desert, desert
Very hot indeed.

Desert, desert
Bigger than you and me.

Desert, desert
Little bugs burrowing.

Desert, desert,
Side winders, side winding.

Desert, desert
Moses and Mohammed were there.

Desert, desert
Older than my great, great, gran.

Joseph Freeman (9)
Terrace Road Primary School, Swansea

Sahara Desert

Desert, desert, hot and long
Crawling insects in the sun.
Desert, desert, growing and shrinking
Desert, desert, fire burning in my heart.
I fall to the ground in tiredness
Water, water
I need water.
The only thing I need
I'll die without it.

Rebekah Ellis (9)
Terrace Road Primary School, Swansea

Desert

Desert, desert, desert
is a life of Hell and Heaven.
Mohammed went there
he said a prayer.
He found Allah
far away in the desert.
Desert, desert,
How will we survive there?
Strangers can help us.
Riverbeds are dry,
We need a well.
So dig one.
We see strange camels
So buy them.
The desert is dangerous.

Sakariya Abdi (9)
Terrace Road Primary School, Swansea

The Sahara Desert

Heat, heat, heat every day.
The sun burning into my skin.
The wind blowing the sand into my face,
No water to drink,
An enormous desert burning my strength to ashes.

Rhys Thomas (10)
Terrace Road Primary School, Swansea

Sahara Desert

The desert is scorching
Like a massive ball of fire,
The sun is melting the orange sand,
Turning it red
Turning it brown,
Making in steam and shimmer.
Sand in dunes,
Dunes high as mountains.
Ripple like the sea,
Stretching to eternity.

Sam Davies (10)
Terrace Road Primary School, Swansea

Sahara

Sahara, Sahara in the sun
Sahara, Sahara all day long
Sahara, Sahara it's no fun
Sahara, Sahara it's so tidy.

Desert, desert like an ocean
Desert, desert changing all the time
Desert, desert deadly and frightening
Desert, desert growing and stretching
Desert, desert like a pathway
Desert, desert roasting and cooking.

Walk on, I must survive
I must survive.
I must survive.
I must survive.

Luke Harris (9)
Terrace Road Primary School, Swansea

Summer - Haiku

The sun is burning,
Children play on the hot beach,
Ice creams are melting.

Belal Ahmad (11)
Tredegarville CW Primary School, Cardiff

Untitled

I had a dream, I was flying up high,
I was lying on a cloud and touching the sky.
I was flying in space and I saw the moon,
I dreamt of a race, but I was waking up soon.
I dreamt of my family, I dreamt of a friend,
This dream was amazing, I didn't want it to end.

Levi Charles (9)
Tredegarville CW Primary School, Cardiff

My Dream

My dream is to sit on a cloud
and explore the night sky,
watch the stars whiz past,
then when all is quiet
I'd jump off the cloud
and into the Milky Way.

Then before I can blink, the
shiny night sky would fade,
and I'd be on a hot island
watching the sun set
and I'd wake up in my bed.

Rachel Cazenave-Smith (10)
Tredegarville CW Primary School, Cardiff

My Dream

My dream for the future would be . . .
to make people be more nice to other people.

My dream for the future would be . . .
to change the world into a nice world.

My dream for the future would be . . .
to stop people from smoking and eating
lots of food with sugar in it.

My dream for the future would be . . .
to get away from Cardiff and live in a hot country.

My dream for the future would be . . .
to sleep all day long!

Danielle Hall (10)
Tredegarville CW Primary School, Cardiff

My Dream

If I had a dream that would change my life
It would be . . .
To run in a great race with
a horse named Ollie.
Running through a desert full
of smoke, blinding my eyes.

Twitching and turning, I woke up,
slowly I get my vision back,
I try to fall back to sleep,
eventually I do.
This time it's different, I'm
in a stable getting ready to race.

Still asleep, we've been racing
for many days and nights.
Coming to the finish line and just before
I get there, I take a breath and
immediately it's all over.

My wish never came true!

Breeze Thompson (10)
Tredegarville CW Primary School, Cardiff

My Dream

My dream of a perfect world would be . . .

That there were no wars and no fighting,
and everyone should just be nice to one another.

My dream of a perfect world would be . . .

That people should speak the same language
so the world could be peaceful.

My dream of a perfect world would be . . .

Lauren Trickett (10)
Tredegarville CW Primary School, Cardiff

Cheerleading - Haiku

Cheerleading is good,
It's one of my favourites.
To me it's the best!

Mica Schiazza (11)
Tredegarville CW Primary School, Cardiff

My Dream

Who would like to have new friends?
Me!
Who would like a talking animal?
Me!
Who would like to see a rainbow every day?
Me!
Who would like to see a beautiful garden?
Me!
Who would like no school anymore?
Me!
Who would like a wonderful year?
Me!
Who would like to have a nice adventure?
Me!
Who would like to be cared for?
Me!

Zahra Chowdhury (8)
Tredegarville CW Primary School, Cardiff

My Dream

I went to my bed and what did I see?
A scary vampire following me.

I went to my school and what did I see?
A giant worksheet in front of me.

I went to the shop and what did I see?
A floating till in front of me.

I went to the shelf and what did I see?
A small fluffy kitten in front of me.

Jacob Charles (8)
Tredegarville CW Primary School, Cardiff

My Dream

One night I had a dream
It was a scary dream,
It was a scary, horrible dream,
It was a scary, horrible, nasty dream.
It was a scary, horrible, nasty, horrifying dream.
It was a scary, horrible, nasty, horrifying, interesting dream.
It was a scary, horrible, nasty, horrifying, interesting, lovely dream.

Michaela Williams (8)
Tredegarville CW Primary School, Cardiff

My Dream

I had a dream and what did I see?
My pets speaking to me.

I had a dream and what did I see?
A lion playing with me.

I had a dream and what did I see?
A crocodile staring at me.

I had a dream and what did I see?
An elephant staring at me.

I had a dream and what did I see?
A blue whale staring at me.

I had dream and what did I see,
A puppy speaking to me.

I had a dream and what did I see,
A cat chasing me.

I had a dream and what did I see?
A snake hissing at me.

Shannon Manfield (8)
Tredegarville CW Primary School, Cardiff

My Dream

I had a dream and what did I see?
The bogeyman chasing me.

I had a dream and what did I see?
Monsters in my closet.

I had a dream and what did I see?
A Dalek following me.

I had a dream and what did I see?
Spiders in my hair.

Joshua Trickett (8)
Tredegarville CW Primary School, Cardiff

My Dream

Who would like to see no school?
Who would like to see a talking cat?
Who would like to see nice rides?
Who would like to see a big pool?
Who would like to see my birthday, every day?
Who would like to see magic fingers?
Who would like to see a Man Utd player?
Who would like to see a real football?
Who would like to see a dragon?
Me!

Corey Stephens (7)
Tredegarville CW Primary School, Cardiff

My Dream

It was a big dog,
It was a fluffy big dog.
It was a slim, fluffy big dog.
It was a hairy, slim, fluffy big dog.
It was a black, hairy, slim, fluffy big dog.
It was a brown, black, hairy, slim, fluffy big dog.
It was a funny, brown, black, hairy, slim, fluffy big dog.

Samantha Carter (8)
Tredegarville CW Primary School, Cardiff

My Dream

I had a dream and what did I see?
A bat flapping at me.
I had a dream and what did I see?
A big bee buzzing at me.
I had a dream and what did I see?
A tiger leaping at me.
I had a dream and what did I see?
A vampire coming at me.
I had a dream and what did I see?
A bear growling at me.
I had a dream and what did I see?
A Dalek staring at me.

Kieran Fitzpatrick (8)
Tredegarville CW Primary School, Cardiff

My Dream

A china doll on a shelf,
spooky, alive,
watching, alive,
very alive.
Pale, pale face,
blinking black eyes.
The creaking of the neck, moving
Creeeeeeeeeeeeeeeeeek!

I walked towards it
tired, but eyes open,
alive, very alive
but sits!
I get closer,
I reach out,
I touch the face.
I woke up, shivering
in my bed.
I looked up, a china doll
with black eyes watching,
alive, very alive!

Rachael Woodrow (11)
Tredegarville CW Primary School, Cardiff

Football - Haiku

Man U are so dumb,
But Liverpool are the best,
Better than the rest.

Talal Hesham Ghrairi (11)
Tredegarville CW Primary School, Cardiff

Football - Haiku

Liverpool are the
Best, they will always beat the
Rest, in a red vest.

Kieren Pash (11)
Tredegarville CW Primary School, Cardiff

Family - Haiku

I have a father,
I have a mother, I have
Two nans, I love them.

Daniel Kilford (10)
Tredegarville CW Primary School, Cardiff

Friend - Haiku

Hello my name is
Atlanta my best friend's name
Is Chelsea. Bye-bye.

Atlanta Hewings (10)
Tredegarville CW Primary School, Cardiff

Football - Haiku

Football is the best,
way better than the rest, so
I play it a lot.

Isaac Kahar (11)
Tredegarville CW Primary School, Cardiff

Dance

In my dream last night,
I was a dancer on the stage,
I love to dance.

Chelsea Copp (11)
Tredegarville CW Primary School, Cardiff

Ice Cream - Haiku

I like ice cream lots,
Vanilla is my favourite.
Chocolate is nice too.

Shanice Burnett (11)
Tredegarville CW Primary School, Cardiff

Family - Haiku

My brother's Kemor
He lives in Barbados with
My dad and sisters.

Natasha Wilkinson (10)
Tredegarville CW Primary School, Cardiff

The Black Widow Spider

The black widow spider crawls slowly around the bright shining sun
as it injects the poison of darkness.
He wraps his black web around the sun and consumes its light.
The Earth is trapped in its predator's shadow.
He crawls around the lands, trailing his dark mist of poison.
You can smell the stench on his sweaty legs.
You can hear nothing but eight gigantic spikes staggering
into the ground.
You can touch nothing but cold misty hairs on the end of
your fingertips.
You can see shadows of spiders crawling upon your house,
Terminating everything in its path.
You can taste the dust of houses as they crumble in the dark.
But this is just a nightmare though, dark is still around.

Joe Paley (11)
Trellech Primary School, Monmouth

Anger

Anger overwhelms me, like a prowling black cat,
The taste is unbearable, of blood and sweat.
I hear screams of torture, explosions and bombs.
I see people and animals dying of cruelty.
The smell of rotting flesh haunts the air like a thick fog.

All I feel is wet cold stone, as I hit the floor,
No sound, no taste, nor smell of raging fire.
I don't see or feel anything anymore,
I have no hope, I'm at Death's door.

Anger is an emotion that burns into your heart,
It hurts family and friends.
Anger overwhelms me
I have no heart.

Abbie Ellicott (11)
Trellech Primary School, Monmouth

Anger

Anger is red, like freshly spilled blood
from an unlucky victim of murder.
It sounds like someone's cries of pain
in a mediaeval dungeon.
It smells like old tyres on a bonfire,
It feels like I'm on fire.
It tastes like trying to suck ten lemons
all at once.
Anger reminds me of fighting
with my friends.

Tom Kedward (11)
Trellech Primary School, Monmouth

Anger

Anger is like a volcano exploding
out of your mouth,
It sounds terrible, people cry
and shake with fear.
As I shake the room with my voice,
I taste fear, but how?
I smell smoke from the fire
and taste blood, trying to stop
by biting my lip.
Then up my spine, a shiver
makes me fall to the ground.
I've stopped -
things are better, I hope.
What have I done?
The anger has won
and has changed me forever.

Bethan Gorvett (11)
Trellech Primary School, Monmouth

The Black Bat

The black bat glides across the sunlit desert
bringing its fine dark mist behind its sharp
hairy back.

It makes people cry and others sigh.
It rips the brightness apart with its
two razor-sharp fangs and makes
a hole so deep that light is no more.

Lakota Gunter (10)
Trellech Primary School, Monmouth

Anger

Anger is as red as a raging fire
it's a curse of hatred and torment.
It can turn the most goodwilled heart
into a burning, horrible, fierce heart.
The stench of anger smells like rotting flesh,
It looks like a fiery volcano spurting up boiling lava.

The sound of it is like people screaming while a
family member is trapped inside a burning building.
It feels as horrible as a thousand scorpions
thrusting their stings into you.
The taste of anger is like eating burning fire,
Anger is the most terrible feeling of all.

Sean McMahon (10)
Trellech Primary School, Monmouth

The Dark Land

Dark, he wears a black cloak,
He is the almighty king of black,
He is invisible to all they call Death,
When he goes past, you can smell the stench
Of blood and see black.
You only hear trees swaying with the motion of the wind.
You can only touch cold.
The taste of damp leaves is around you,
His face is hidden under his hood, evil and rotten.
But then light shines for the start of the day,
He goes back to his domain,
But remember, Death is still around.

Ben Hyde (11)
Trellech Primary School, Monmouth

The Anger Queen

Anger is bright, like a terrifying firework,
She sounds hurtful, like a bull.
She smells like a rotting warehouse,
She feels cold slabs, like ice beneath her feet.
She tastes blood and sweat like it was her food,
Suddenly you see red smoke like a roaring fire,
Anger will always pierce your heart.

Gabrielle Jones (11)
Trellech Primary School, Monmouth

Darkness

The spooky darkness brings day to an end,
All those things out there we'll have to defend.
You walk outside and get a fright,
But all it is, is the black of night.
Standing still, you look around,
You can't even see the frozen ground,
You can smell tremendous charcoal burning,
You feel as though the Earth is turning.
The dawn is breaking -
Through all your strength, you are learning,
Although the darkness is still there,
You know the darkness is never dead.

Emily Kedward (10)
Trellech Primary School, Monmouth

Darkness

As soon as light has gone,
The darkness floods in again.
Some people scare with tears in the darkness of night,
You can't see through his pitch-black body.
His horrible touch sends a shiver down your back.
The coldness of his breath seeps through your body,
Making you colder and colder until you freeze stiff,
And the taste of rotten leaves fall from the trees.
The smell of damp air slithers up your nose,
As soon as dawn breaks, the light floods in.

Sam Land (10)
Trellech Primary School, Monmouth

Anger

Anger looks like a family suffering in pain,
When you hear anger, you hear punishment and death.
He feels pain all the time,
You will always taste fear
And you will sometimes smell anger.

Andrew Morgan (10)
Trellech Primary School, Monmouth

Darkness

Darkness is the night-time beast,
It only comes out when you hear its call,
It whispers to you when you're in your bed,
You cannot see it as it is all black.
All I can feel is the darkness of the night.
I can smell fear and it's very near.
I can taste the damp air rushing in
Through my window.
I look around, it was all just a terrible dream.

Nicola Bowen (11)
Trellech Primary School, Monmouth

Anger

The dragon inside awakens,
His hot fire, boils my blood.
A red mist descends, fogging my vision,
Blinding reason and judgement.
He roars, rattling my eardrums,
Pounding on my chest.
I feel his claws clutching at my heart.
I taste ash burning on my tongue.
Suddenly it stops.
Growling he descends back to his lair,
Returning to his slumbers,
Leaving behind horror and destruction.

Liam Musselbrook (11)
Trellech Primary School, Monmouth

Anger

Anger is an evil spirit that controls your life,
He feels like a razor-sharp knife.
He's like a raging bonfire or an angry ghoul.
He's a fire-breathing dragon, destroying all.
You hear him roaring, loud as a raging storm,
He digs in sharp like a jagged thorn,
Everybody fears him burning inside,
Everyone runs and tries to hide.
Anger is evil, deadly and full of fright.
He'll rip you up with all his might.

Harry King (11)
Trellech Primary School, Monmouth

Darkness Of The Night

The darkness of the night is when you switch off the light
and you run to your bed.
You feel something behind you,
you cover your head,
the awful smell of fright looms in the air.
You taste the cold air which sends a shiver down your spine.
The wind batters on your window.
You see a figure by the stairs,
your heart has got faster,
you feel so scared.
You wake up, you look around,
you were never there!

Zoe Horsfield (10)
Trellech Primary School, Monmouth

Darkness

He comes in the day and shadows the door,
He blots out the sun 'til light is no more.
You can sense him there by the door,
You can taste your fear, your mouth is dry,
You can feel his eyes, so extremely sly,
You can hear his breath whistling by,
He's coming, it's time for day to die.

Tom Kelly (10)
Trellech Primary School, Monmouth

Happiness

Happiness is like a hot summer's day with the wind on your face
Happiness tastes like a creamy chocolate fudge cake with ice cream
Happiness looks like a first born kitten in a nice, warm basket
Happiness sounds like a robin singing a lovely sweet song
Happiness reminds me of my family tree
Happiness is the greatest emotion in the entire world
Happiness can change your life.

Bethan King (8)
Trellech Primary School, Monmouth

Anger

Anger is like a black hooded figure
Anger is a colossal battlefield under the cold moonlight
Anger feels like an ambush springing out of the darkness
Anger looks like a ring of scorching flames
Anger smells like a rotting corpse
Anger sounds like a hissing enormous snake
Anger tastes like blood filling your lungs
Anger is like a never ending corridor
Anger is terrifying.

Stephanie Warner (9)
Trellech Primary School, Monmouth

Anger

Anger is like red-hot lava pouring out of a volcano
Anger is a colossal flame dancing as a monster in the dark
Anger feels like a hound ripping a hare to pieces
Anger looks like a ring of vampire bats
Anger sounds like a hissing cobra
Anger smells like a rotting corpse
Anger tastes like blood trickling from a person's throat
Anger is terrifying.

Lianne Edwards (9)
Trellech Primary School, Monmouth

Love

Love is a wonderful feeling,
You get it when you are round people,
Love is the colour of red,
It smells of sweet red roses,
Tastes of hot malting chocolate,
It sounds like birds singing
And looks like lambs playing.

Edward Land (8) & Robert Bowen (8)
Trellech Primary School, Monmouth

Happiness

Happiness is the angel that sings.
Happiness is the light of goodness.
Happiness is the sound of laughter.
Happiness reminds me of celebration.
Happiness reminds me of the colour blue.
Happiness reminds me of playing games.
Happiness reminds me of the warm sun.

Matthew Casson (9)
Trellech Primary School, Monmouth

The Darkness

Darkness is good,
Darkness is bad,
Darkness is where the Devil went mad.

Darkness is scary,
The floorboards creak,
You walk into the darkness and see a zombie peek.

You slip on the floorboard
And bang your head,
'Time to die,' the zombie said.

Morgan Paley (9)
Trellech Primary School, Monmouth

Love

Love is nice, love is sweet
Love encourages hearts to beat
Eve loved Adam, Adam loved Eve
Love is like Christmas Eve.

Love feels like pillows
It looks like puppies
And do you know what . . .
It's as quiet as guppies.

Love blazes like bonfires
And runs like the wind
It's as big as the seas
And never gets binned.

Love is fun, love is great
Love is like fresh cookies baked
Some loves are deep, some are shallow
But we've learned something . . . that love is marshmallow.

Daniel Musselbrook (9)
Trellech Primary School, Monmouth

Anger

Anger feels like a deep pain inside you
It tastes bitter and sour inside you
It looks like the Devil himself
It sounds like an evil cackle
It smells like a boiling hot smoking bonfire
It's anger.

Christopher Widdicks (9)
Trellech Primary School, Monmouth

Sadness

Sadness is like rain falling from big black clouds in the sky
Sadness sounds like babies crying
Sadness tastes like murky water
Sadness is like your worst enemy
Sadness smells like smoke
Sadness is like having a bad day.

Briony Waycott (9)
Trellech Primary School, Monmouth

Happiness

Happiness is pink like chewing gum,
Happiness tastes like Sunday roast,
Happiness looks like a nice friendly face,
Happiness reminds me of my birthday,
Happiness sounds like my mum telling a story,
Happiness smells like air.

Bethany Powell (8)
Trellech Primary School, Monmouth

Happiness

Happiness is orange like a juicy orange,
It tastes like sweet fluffy candyfloss,
It smells like sticky toffee,
It looks like a cute fluffy kitten,
It sounds like sizzling sausages,
It looks like runny chocolate,
It reminds me of the day I had a new teacher.

Kirsten Jeffs (7)
Trellech Primary School, Monmouth

Happiness

Happiness is golden like toffee,
It looks like golden wrapping paper,
It tastes like toffee,
It sounds like a gentle breeze,
It smells like a rose,
It reminds me of daisies,
It feels like a fluffy dog.

Thomas Bristow (8)
Trellech Primary School, Monmouth

Fun

Fun is red like a football kit,
It tastes like a goodie bag full of rainbow drops,
It looks like someone scoring the winning goal,
Fun feels like jumping on air,
It sounds like the roar of the crowd.

Bradd Morgan-Bowen (9)
Trellech Primary School, Monmouth

Happiness

Happiness is yellow like a bright summer sun,
It tastes like sharp lemon ice cream,
It looks like beautiful dogs running around all together,
It sounds like laughter of happy, cheerful people,
It smells like the sweet smell of melted chocolate,
It reminds me of the bright summer holidays,
It feels like fluffy teddies on my bed.

Emily Pardington (8)
Trellech Primary School, Monmouth

Happiness

Happiness is red and orange like the shining sun,
It looks like children playing happily in the playground,
It sounds like a puppy barking for food,
It smells like chocolate melting in the sun,
It feels like soft fluffy fur on a cute looking dog,
It tastes like sweet vanilla ice cream,
It reminds me of sweets in a row ready to be eaten.

Emily Pettitt (8)
Trellech Primary School, Monmouth

Fun

Fun is yellow like a big bright sun,
It tastes like bright lollipops,
It looks like a huge blue sky above,
It sounds like laughing children when they are playing
It smells like sweet lemon ice cream in a bowl,
It feels like golden sticky toffee in my fingers,
It reminds me of loads of chocolate melting together.

Alice Pettitt (8)
Trellech Primary School, Monmouth

Fear

Fear is red like lava pouring out of volcanoes.
It reminds me of the red colour of my bedroom.
It smells like smoke from the fires.
It looks like sparkling rubies.
It sounds like blowing red fire.
It tastes like strawberry candyfloss.
It feels like rough bricks.

Joshua Rodgers (8)
Trellech Primary School, Monmouth

Fun

Fun is yellow like lemon sherbets.
It tastes like lemons.
It looks like the sun in the sky.
It reminds me of a big fire fun day.
It sounds like rockets going zoom.
It smells like sweets.
It feels like a big soft cloud.

Kitty Jones (8)
Trellech Primary School, Monmouth

Anger

Anger is red like a volcano erupting in the sky.
It feels like fire blazing.
It tastes like boiling hot chilli.
It smells like ashes from a volcano.
It reminds me of fizzy Coke.
It looks like a burning skyscraper.
It sounds like a wolf howling to the moon.

George Burnett (7)
Trellech Primary School, Monmouth

The Pop Artist

His long black hair lops on his shoulders
Like a plank of wood falling from far away lands.
His cheeks are just hollow ditches in his face,
His eyes are sunken in through dark glasses,
His hands clutched tight to the cold microphone,
His body, thin as a rake,
His skin, pale as snow,
His voice, quiet as a mouse.

Hannah Pockett (10)
Tutshill CE Primary School, Chepstow

Treasure Bag

What shall I find in my bag today?
A curled up page from a pirate book?
I wonder who's lost it, maybe it's Hook?
I want to know what else there is, dare I look?
I'll just stroke outside it to see what I feel . . .
Is it my imagination or is it real?
I think I feel a sharp gold tooth,
Shall I open it to see the proof?
Maybe today I'll leave it alone
And imagine the treasures that are left unknown.

Sophie Piccirilli (9)
Tutshill CE Primary School, Chepstow

Wolves

Wolves are furry
Wolves are fluffy
They have eyes as green as the grass
They live in the wild
They have claws as sharp as shark teeth
Whilst they run through the wild the rain can't touch them
They surround their prey as the other animal asks for help
Wolves are furry
And they are fluffy.

Jack Fear (9)
Tutshill CE Primary School, Chepstow

The Witch's Dessert!

What shall I put in my dessert today?
A tasty chocolate bar,
A pixie wing,
A jewel stolen from a king
And a pickle from a jar.
A pound of butter,
A slice of bread,
A ballerina too.
A girlie plait
And some of that
And a pot full of stew.
A hairy toe,
A couple of fingers
And the voices stolen from the cowboy singers.
A silver slipper,
A bowl of jelly
And Channel One off the telly.
An English book,
A rabbit I took,
And I stole the carrot too.
A dotty jumper,
A Rollerblade
And a suitcase full of aid.
A bright coloured rose,
A hair bobble
And a fairy that's nothing but trouble.
A busy bee,
A stolen key
And a piece of paper too.
I think that shall do,
Do you want some too?

Katie Burton (9) & Jessie Calway (10)
Tutshill CE Primary School, Chepstow

The Fairy Land

One day when I was on the beach,
We bought a picnic,
We had some fruit - apples, pears and a peach.
I got bored and wandered and what did I find?

A magical land, a fairy land,
I could not believe my eyes as fairies rushed by,
Inside a cave with a soft carpet of sand,
It was like a special glade.

And at the back sat a fairy on a throne
Of seaweed and of shells,
She was the prettiest fairy anyone had ever seen,
But when it was time to go I could not leave this land.

But I came back again and again
But there was no fairyland,
Just a cave and lots and lots of sand.

Beth Donaldson (9)
Tutshill CE Primary School, Chepstow

Pasta

Pasta, pasta
It's wonderful stuff
Pasta, pasta
I can't get enough

Pasta, pasta
You are so great
Pasta, pasta
You're served on a plate

Pasta, pasta
With tomato sauce
Pasta, pasta
You're my favourite course

Pasta, pasta
Can I have some please?
Pasta, pasta
With ham and cheese

Pasta, pasta
You're my favourite dish
Pasta, pasta
You are delish.

Emma Watson & Georgia Bannard (9)
Tutshill CE Primary School, Chepstow

Whizz Pop

Faster than fairies
Faster than witches
Over the hills
And under the ditches
Through the mountains
Around the hills
Watch out, there it goes.

Eve Walton (10)
Tutshill CE Primary School, Chepstow

Remote Race

And the race is on,
In the blue team it's Sam,
In the red, the champion so far, Holly!
So, will the blue team win and get to watch Lost,
Or the red team who'll watch Tracy Beaker?
Who will get the remote first?
Sam reaches for the remote, but he's too slow,
Holly has slipped through his legs and snatched it first.
As Holly flicks through the channels, Sam quickly gets her
in a headlock.

Is it all over?
No it isn't!
Holly is back in the game,
Just as Sam kicks her in the bum, Mum walks in.
He is grounded.
And the red team have won.

Holly Riordan (9)
Tutshill CE Primary School, Chepstow

Gym

On the bar you can swing like a monkey.
On the floor you can flip as high as a grasshopper.
On the beam you can cartwheel all along it.
On the trampoline you can jump as high as a horse.
On the vault you can leap as fast as a frog.
I like gym because there is lots to do.

Nicole Dyson (10)
Tutshill CE Primary School, Chepstow

Max Meets A Creep

Max meets a terrible creep
Max, Max didn't weep
The creep was slimy, the creep was scary
The creep's big feet were big and hairy,
'Hello Max, good day to you,
How shall I eat up you?'
Max, Max didn't worry
Max didn't scream or scurry
He washed his hands
And slicked back his hair
Then ate the monster up
As quick as a bear.

Alex Heaton (9)
Tutshill CE Primary School, Chepstow

Tigers

Tiger! Tiger having a fight,
In the deep black night,
He hit a punch
And got back a bunch (painful).

Tiger! Tiger orange and black,
Tiger's mercy their only lack,
Tiger's roar trembles the Earth,
They are vulnerable at their birth.

Tiger! Tiger always so fast,
Sabre-toothed ancestors from the past,
Tigers hunting their speciality,
They'll eat anything in reality.

Tiger! Tiger racing and racing,
Getting angry, pacing and pacing,
Gets a whiff of his prey,
A squirrel it is for today.

David Monk (9)
Tutshill CE Primary School, Chepstow

The Wicked Witch

When all the town was sleeping
And the wizard had gone to bed,
Out flew a witch, and this is what she said,

'I'm a wicked, wicked witch
with a dingle-dangle hat,
I can turn around like this
And flip around like that.'

My black cat fell asleep
By my dingle-dangle feet,
Out flew a witch and shouted very loud,

'I'm a wicked, wicked witch
with a dingle-dangle hat,
I can turn around like this
And flip around like that.'

Beth Childs (10)
Tutshill CE Primary School, Chepstow

Tiger, Tiger

Tiger, tiger in the street,
Tiger, tiger roaring beat,
Tiger, tiger behind a tree,
Tiger, tiger looking at me,
Tiger, tiger in the wild,
Tiger, tiger eating a child,
Tiger, tiger in the night,
Tiger, tiger having a fright,
Tiger, tiger in the wild,
Tiger, tiger cleaning its child,
Tiger, tiger in the lake,
Tiger, tiger, luring its bait.

Davey Wilkinson Lessels (10)
Tutshill CE Primary School, Chepstow

Cheetah, Cheetah

Cheetah, cheetah
In the sun,
Cheetah, cheetah
Look at him run.

Cheetah, cheetah
In the heat,
Cheetah, cheetah
Eating his meat.

Cheetah, cheetah
In a boat,
Cheetah, cheetah
Can you float?

Cheetah, cheetah
Hunting his prey,
Cheetah, cheetah
Has found a way.

Cheetah, cheetah
Caught the deer,
Cheetah, cheetah's
Lunch is here.

Corey Fieldhouse & James Calverley (10)
Tutshill CE Primary School, Chepstow

A Poem To Be Spoken Silently

It was so quiet that I heard a rock tapping.
It was so quiet that I heard the air swishing.
It was so quiet that I heard the flowers growing.
It was so quiet that I heard a pencil roll on my hand.
It was so quiet that I heard a bird flying.
It was so quiet that I heard the worms sliding in the mud.
It was so quiet I heard the sun shining.
It was so quiet that I heard the sand hitting the water.

Elizabeth Topley (7) & Elinor Lovering (8)
Tutshill CE Primary School, Chepstow

Nature's Numbers

One old, observant owl,
Two turtles trick or treating,
Three tickled tigers,
Four fantastic fish,
Five famous frogs,
Six silly sausages,
Seven smelly sharks,
Eight exercising elephants,
Nine naughty newts,
Ten terrifying trout.

Jack Prince (7)
Tutshill CE Primary School, Chepstow

A Poem To Be Spoken Silently

It was so quiet
That I heard the bunnies hop.
It was so quiet
That I heard the snow drop.
It was so quiet
That I heard someone touch my glasses.

Ella Bailey (8)
Tutshill CE Primary School, Chepstow

A Poem To Be Spoken Silently

It was so quiet
That I heard raindrops falling from the sky.
It was so quiet
That I heard birds gliding across the sky.
It was so quiet
That I heard the roses grow.
It was so quiet
That I heard the Earth spin.

Amy Bradley (7)
Tutshill CE Primary School, Chepstow

A Poem To Be Spoken Silently

It was so quiet
That I heard the squeak of a mouse.
It was so quiet
That I heard raindrops fall to the ground.
It was so quiet
That I heard the magic.
It was so quiet
That I heard the Earth go round in circles.
It was so quiet
That I heard an eagle swoop across the sky.

Bryonnie Jones (8)
Tutshill CE Primary School, Chepstow

A Poem To Be Spoken Silently

It was so quiet
That I heard my fish swim in the tank.
It was so quiet
That I heard the roses growing.
It was so quiet
That I heard snowflakes falling to the ground.
It was so quiet
That I heard my hair swishing.

Sarah-Jayne Blatchly (7)
Tutshill CE Primary School, Chepstow

A Poem To Be Spoken Silently

It was so quiet
I heard drops coming out of the tap.
It was so quiet
I could hear my hair grow.
It was so quiet
That I heard a butterfly wing flapping.
It was so quiet
That I heard leaves fall off the tree.

Christopher Dewhurst-Trigg (7)
Tutshill CE Primary School, Chepstow

Sky

The sky is so high,
The clouds make a picture of a pie.
The sky is so big,
Covering the Earth like a wig.
The sky is grey
Every day in the UK.
Why is the sky so high?
So we can all fly.

Max Neale (9)
Tutshill CE Primary School, Chepstow

Rabbit, Rabbit

Rabbit, rabbit, in the night,
In the morning it will be light.
Don't you dare even fight,
Because your coat won't be white.
Rabbit you are a pretty sight.
Rabbit, rabbit off you hop,
If you eat too much you'll pop.
You are better than a friend,
I will play with you each weekend.

Amy Connor (9)
Tutshill CE Primary School, Chepstow

Mother Nature

Look at the flowers above my door,
Oh, they look so beautiful.
Use the light so you can see,
See what you are meant to be.

Why do people crush and stand,
When you can just enjoy the land?
Looking round to see the trees
And maybe even bumblebees.

Nature, nature, all around,
Even up and on the ground.
Next time you make a daisy chain,
Don't forget nature's honest grain.

Carly Burt (10)
Tutshill CE Primary School, Chepstow

Pups

Puppies, puppies everywhere
People stop, people stare
Fluffy and soft, black and white
Bark, bark, all the night.

Digging holes in the ground
Oh no, what have they found?
Mud and stones flying high
Look out birds flying by!

Walkies, walkies, they love them so
Round the fields and off they go
Meeting friends along the way
Oh what fun, they love to play.

Dinnertime is a dash
Dishes fly with a crash
Then it's time for a nap
Give those pups a great big clap.

They are such a naughty lot
Biting all the things we've got
They look so cute it's hard to shout
They wonder what it's all about.

They run and dart around my feet
It must be time for a treat
Biscuits go one by one
And don't forget one for their mum.

Now it's time to go to bed
In their kennel in the shed
They cuddle up, nice and tight
Asleep until the morning light.

Soon it'll be time to leave their mum
New homes are ready, oh what fun
They look so fine in all their glory
And this is the end of my story.

Lucie Norris (10)
Tutshill CE Primary School, Chepstow

Beach Day

When I go to the beach . . .
I sail the waves,
Maybe even sunbathe.

When I go to the beach . . .
I bury myself in sand
The little grains
Feel like insects between my toes.

When I go to the beach . . .
I dig massive holes
I pour water in them
I look away, then look back . . .
And the water has vanished.

Kelsey Thomas (11)
Tutshill CE Primary School, Chepstow

Masai Mara!

The sun rises into the
Hot dawning of Africa.

Giraffes trudge through
The long, thick grass.
Hippos grumble in the midday sun.

The lion roars in the sunlight,
While the cubs clamber over their mother
And eagles fly overhead.

The men secure the village camp with thorny fences.
Elephants bathe in the waterholes,
Beside the pink flamingos.

Zebra and antelope graze side by side,
Together in their need to survive.
Hyenas give out a cackle to warn others around them.
Monkeys swing from tree to tree!

The sun sets in Africa.
The sky burns like a fire
And all is peaceful once again!

Rebecca Shiner (10)
Tutshill CE Primary School, Chepstow

Big Elephant

I think I'll be a huge elephant,
So proud and nearly intelligent.
No hound or snake will come near me,
Because I will squish them like a pea.
I plod all day
And I sleep all night.
I scratched my bum on a tree
To get rid of that pesky flea!

Daniel Bailey (10)
Tutshill CE Primary School, Chepstow

Wolf's Rage!

His eyes are like the moonlit sky,
His coat of a shining silver, that I can't deny.
His breath like the air that surrounds us.
The wolf stands there, as if waiting for a bus!
But then, as if from nowhere,
A sudden rage fills the air.
His moonlit eyes start to turn red
As he chases you he looks hot in the head!
And when he catches you, you'll know it all right,
As the air goes cold around you in the night.
And I still remember, even at my age,
The cold night I escaped *the wolf's rage*.

Mathew Hoare (11)
Tutshill CE Primary School, Chepstow

The Countryside

The countryside is a very pleasant place to be,
It is so peaceful and quiet and full of wide open space.
You can smell the sweet, lush green grass in the air.
The deep, dark forest can be viewed from afar.
You can hear the tractors roaring up through the valleys.
The rolling hills are a part of the landscape.
The smell of the wild flowers is so beautiful.
You can sense the presence of the wild animals around you.
What a lucky person I am to live in the countryside,
It's such a beautiful place to be.

Benjamin Price-Williams (10)
Tutshill CE Primary School, Chepstow

Reminds Me Of My Mum

Mums are wise, mums are clever,
My mum will be with me forever.
In all the things I do each day,
I know she's with me all the way.

If I fall down or get hurt playing rugby,
There's always one person who's there to look after me.
She knows all the things I like to eat,
Chocolate, pancakes are a particular treat!

When bedtime comes she gives me a cuddle,
Then it's up the stairs 'at the double'.
'Go straight to sleep,' she'll always say,
But sometimes I sneak a little play!

Then in my dreams I stop a while
To think about my mother's smile.
Now these things are said and done,
They all remind me of my mum.

Lewis Beavis (10)
Tutshill CE Primary School, Chepstow

Sunset

As the sun goes down in the evening sky,
I say a long and last goodbye,
As I do, I start to cry,
For I cannot wait for tomorrow.

The colour of red
Fills my head,
And I keep this in mind for I know
The sunset is going to go.

The sun's giant rays go round and round,
But as they fade, you hear a sound,
The sound of joy and glee
That I unleash in me.

Ross Barnett (11)
Tutshill CE Primary School, Chepstow

A Poem To Be Spoken Silently

It was so quiet
That I heard the sun rise.
It was so quiet
That I heard a hedgehog sniff.
It was so quiet
That I heard the clouds move.
It was so quiet
That I heard my hair grow.
It was so quiet
That I heard the birds putting their nests together.
It was so quiet
That I heard the bunnies bouncing in the spring grass.

Isabel Peart (8)
Tutshill CE Primary School, Chepstow

Posing Poems

One ocean otter,
Two talented, tickling tigers,
Three thundering theatres,
Four fantastically fierce fingers,
Five fidgeting, final fingernails,
Six single singing sisters,
Seven sentence September services,
Eight early earthquakes,
Nine knowing nanas,
Ten terrifying terrible twins.

Bethan Evans (8)
Tutshill CE Primary School, Chepstow

A Poem To Be Spoken Silently

It was so quiet
That I heard the growing of the spring leaves.
It was so quiet
That I heard the flutter of a butterfly.
It was so quiet
That I heard the squirrel dig out an acorn.
It was so quiet
That I heard the hatching of a baby bird.
It was so quiet
That I heard the first flower pop through the earth.

Fiona Lovering (8)
Tutshill CE Primary School, Chepstow

Naughty Numbers

One ordinary orange octopus,
Two tall trees,
Three throated thrushes,
Four fantastic frogs,
Five fat fish,
Six small sandwiches,
Seven silly songs,
Eight enormous eggs,
Nine knitting needles,
Ten talking tortoises.

Henry Blight (8)
Tutshill CE Primary School, Chepstow

Love

L ove everyone around you,
O thers that are mean, don't love.
V ery kind people have lots of love.
E veryone has a bit of love in them.

Nicole Rhodes (9)
Tutshill CE Primary School, Chepstow

Nature's Numbers

One odd octopus operating one old owl,
Two ticklish tigers tickling a talented tortoise,
Three thoughtful thieves,
Four fantastically famous frogs,
Five fierce fireworks,
Six sick sandcastles,
Seven sneezy snakes,
Eight elephants eating eggs,
Nine nannies knitting knickers,
Ten tumbling turtles.

Hannah Hobbs (8)
Tutshill CE Primary School, Chepstow

King Arthur And The Round Table

King Arthur had a table which was round
And it only cost a pound.
Every knight had a seat,
Because they never had a defeat.
Every time they had a quest,
They would always do their best.
Every time they met a witch,
They would throw her in the ditch.
Every time they met a wizard
They would throw him in a blizzard.
Every time they wanted a meal they ate a fish
And they served it on a golden dish.
When there was a battle they had all the glory,
That's the end of King Arthur's story.

George Shepherd (9)
Tutshill CE Primary School, Chepstow

Penguin

Deep blue sea,
Cold iceberg,
Smooth black skin,
Fish world,
Winter fish,
Penguin.

Samuel Calway (7)
Tutshill CE Primary School, Chepstow

A Poem To Be Spoken Silently

It was so quiet I could hear
the wind rushing through the air.
It was so quiet I could hear
a fly a million miles away.
It was so quiet I could hear
my hair blowing.

Gabriel Davies (7)
Tutshill CE Primary School, Chepstow

Box Of Dreams

There was a rainbow box
By the side of my bed
I opened it, then
There was swirling mist
All the colours of the rainbow

There I saw my dream
Dolphins jumping in the sea
Then my dream changed to another
Furry kittens running in the sunshine
My dream changed again
Cute little puppies playing in the house
Bang!

My dreams changed again
Sweet rabbits hopping along in the night
Last dream came
A peaceful and happy world

Then the box closed
Ready for another day.

Kelsey Jones (10)
Ysgol Cynlais, Swansea

My Box Of Dreams

My magical multicoloured box
With shining stars
Glimmering glitter on the lid
My box has no particular shape

When I open my box
All these colours emerge
Stars are shooting
Envelopes floating

I was happy holding the cup
All these stallions looked beautiful
All my exams were successful
Our gang going to see Green Day

All my dreams are gone
For another night
The glimmering, glittering top
Goes on my beautiful box.

Amy Jones (10)
Ysgol Cynlais, Swansea

My Box Of Dreams

Under my bed is a box
It is a glittery pink box
With shiny silver stars
And golden moons on it.
I open my box,
A glittering, purple, swirling
Mist appears,
A puff of glitter comes out.
All my magical dreams
Float around me.
There are white ponies,
Prancing and dancing
On the clean green grass,
A sparkling waterfall,
Children playing in the water.
I close my box of dreams
For it to be opened
Another night.

Tanya Burgess (10)
Ysgol Cynlais, Swansea

My Box Of Dreams

My box lies by my head
My box is golden
Always shining
With sparkling stars
On one side
I open my box
White swirling mist appears
I hear
Laughter and robins singing
People getting along with each other
No weapons or bombs

Then I close my box
All the mist disappears
I then put my box
Under my bed
For another night.

Luke Edwards (11)
Ysgol Cynlais, Swansea

Box Of Dreams

My golden, glittering box
Is on the bedside table
I approach the box
I open the box

My golden, glittering box
Releases my dreams
With a clatter

My golden, glittering box
I see dolphins having peace
I see peace at last
I see no war or fighting

My golden, glittering box
I close my box
All my dreams vanish
I hope
I open my box another night.

Kieran Harper (10)
Ysgol Cynlais, Swansea

My Box Of Dreams

My square brown box
When opened
Lots of blood-red ribbons
Shoot out
From inside
Small, sparkling stones
I see my family in the future
I look in my box
Whenever I am sad
Inside is magical
I close it then I open it again
Then I see a white Heaven
Full of angels
I see God talking
With other people
He is talking about their past
Suddenly everything disappears
I put the box back in my drawer
For another day.

Cameron Harkness (10)
Ysgol Cynlais, Swansea

My Box Of Dreams

My mysterious box
Lies at the end of my bed
It is shining
It shimmers in the sun
It's decorated in multicoloured silk
That covers the shine
Of the golden box

When I open the box
A spiralling mist streams out
In an array of colours
Stardust pours out
Shining silver into my eyes
To reveal my wishes and dreams

I see baby lambs grazing in the freshly cut green grass
Children happily playing in the peaceful street
Happy families across the world
To score the winning goal in a tense football match
No bombs, no guns, no more war
Just peace and harmony across the world

I decide to seal my dreams
But only for today
I'll open them another time
But on another day.

Jools Jordan-Probert (10)
Ysgol Cynlais, Swansea

My Box Of Dreams

My box of dreams is under my bed,
Decorated with the Welsh flag,
Photos of my family on the side.
I open it,
Red, white and green mist
Streams out, I look very carefully.
I see myself
In the Millennium Stadium
Scoring tries for Wales.
The red, white and green steam
Sits back down in my box.
I close my box for another time.

Rhys Evans (11)
Ysgol Cynlais, Swansea

My Box Of Dreams

My old, square, antique box
Edges plated in black-painted steel
Locked by an old, rusty key.

I open the box
Gold and orange sparks soar into the air
They blow the door off its hinges
I hear air horns blowing
Crowds cheering
Up flies a thick white cloud
It hovers steadily
It shows Shane Williams playing as captain

Running along side touch
Scoring a try
Wales win at full time
Now it skips to Shane Williams
Holding the silver, gleaming cup high

Everything disappears behind red sparks
And thick green smoke
Everything, even the box.

Josh Evans (11)
Ysgol Cynlais, Swansea

My Box Of Dreams

By the side of my bed
There is a silver box
Covered by shimmering glitter
I go to open it . . .

When opened
Fairies shoot out
Coloured fairy dust follows them
I see a sea of dreams
In that sea of dreams I see . . .

Me at the Commonwealth Games
Then going on to the Olympics
Then to coach Great Britain
I close the box and it all stops
Back to reality.

Nia Lewis (11)
Ysgol Cynlais, Swansea

My Box Of Dreams

My box of dreams
Under my bed there is a small glass box
That is my box of dreams
Dreams is written upon it in gold
Decorated in a rainbow of jewels
My box of dreams

My box of dreams
When I open my box
Thick, sparkling, white mist engulfs me
I fall through it once more
And into my perfect world
My box of dreams

My box of dreams
I see a world without weapons
Without war and poverty
A world where everyone is treated the same
Where peace and happiness is in the air
My box of dreams

My box of dreams
My special box is very fine
But very unpredictable
With a bang I am sucked back
Onto my bed, dreams end for one night
My box of dreams.

Ffion Jenkins (10)
Ysgol Cynlais, Swansea

Box Of Dreams

I have a little
Wooden box
Decorated brightly
With a silky ribbon wrapped around
My box is blue

As I open my tiny box
Bright, illuminating light appears
I hear joy, laughter
And peace
In my pretty box

In my minute box
Is see children playing in a park
I see peace, no war or hatred
I see harmony, no harm
To any life

I see mist covering my dreams
I close my miniature box
I say goodbye
Until another day.

Kaya Main (10)
Ysgol Cynlais, Swansea

Box Of Dreams

I approach the box.
I open the odd-looking box.
A thunderous boom comes out,
A shockwave knocks me backwards.
Electricity comes out with a zap,
It flashes then it finishes.
I then look in the box
And what I see, I watch full of glee.
A boy in the dinosaur age,
Which is me,
Ruler of life,
No extinction,
Sand as bright and rich as the sun
Gleams with the ocean.
Like brothers.
Dinosaurs feeding in the forest,
Perfect camouflage the forest gives.
They evolve into greater humans that can be.
Oh, but what an honour that would be,
Rather than just see.

It then makes a spiral mist
A flash so bright
I cannot open my eye,
Not one bit.
Wind blows in my face
I hear a roar.
I then fall asleep on the floor.
I wake up and find
A fossil to study.

Luke Colamazza (10)
Ysgol Cynlais, Swansea

My Box Of Dreams

My box of dreams is
Blue and pink
Made from marble
Brightly coloured
Decorated with sequins.

When I open my box
A mist is swirling
Colours appear
Butterflies are flying.

My dream is
Being a nurse
Being a singer
For the world to be happy
My dream, my dream, my dream.

When I close my box
My dream is gone
My dream has disappeared
Into Heaven
It has floated with the wind
It's gone, it's gone, it's gone.

Jessica Whiteley (11)
Ysgol Cynlais, Swansea

My Box Of Dreams

In my bedroom
Holding my multicoloured box
That's precious to me
It has silver jewels
Encrusted on the lid
I love my box

I open my box
Beautiful golden hearts
Sprinkle out
Glittering mist swirls around me

I see dolphins playing together
Rabbits jumping in the sun
Waterfalls shining
Children playing happily
I see nice things

Dreams start to fade
Suddenly a star pops out
I catch it
My box disappears
I still hold my star
I will always keep my star.

Stacey Morgan (11)
Ysgol Cynlais, Swansea

My Box Of Dreams

By my bed there is a little box.
It is magnificent and wonderful.
It is so fantastic.
There are stars, glitter covered with rainbows
And gold sequins.
Multicoloured box with gold.

When you open it there is blue mist,
Flowers in the trees,
Red hearts with orange sparkles,
Incredible sunshine,
Pretty stars,
Wonderful sequins.

Baby rabbits with fluffy tails,
The smell of lavender,
The smell of spring,
Peace to the world,
People hugging,
People who have friends,
Coloured people and white people living in peace,
People who have freedom,
People won't be afraid to say their name.

My dreams and wishes can't last long.
The lid hovers across the room and back on my box
And fades away,
My dreams sleep away,
My box leaves behind a star and that makes me happy.

Katy Broad (11)
Ysgol Cynlais, Swansea

How We Sometimes Feel

Anger
Anger is black,
It tastes like red-hot chilli peppers,
It smells like bad breath,
It looks like a tornado,
It sounds like a roaring dragon,
It feels like rough sandpaper.
Anger is evil.

Happiness
Happiness is yellow.
It tastes like boiled sweets,
It smells like fresh air,
It looks like a field of poppies,
It sounds like classical music,
It feels like a soft blanket.
Happiness is stars in the sky.

Love
Love tastes like red jelly and ice cream.
It smells like red roses,
It looks like hearts on a Valentine card,
It sounds like church bells ringing,
It feels like soft lips kissing.
Love is beautiful.

Logan Spittle (9)
Ysgol Cynlais, Swansea

Box Of Dreams

In my room under an old cloth there is a box
But this is not just a 'box'
It's full of my dreams
My desires
It's an old, black wooden chest
With silver-lined sides, a silver, bell-shaped lock
But there's no key
It opens when I want it to

When I open it
Bang!
A huge, silent, shining, harmless tornado

Flies out
Little blue sparks whizz around giggling
A purple winding vortex that spins
Into my first dream . . .

A forest
But not just a forest
A forest with no sharp, evil chainsaws
No lumbering, smelly diggers
Or toxic fumes
But men growing trees

Whoosh . . .
My second dream
Has arrived
An army
But an army destroying their weapons
Taking apart missiles
And vile guns
The picture fades
And a green car appears

The car pulls into a drive
And a little girl runs out
Into the house next to mine
Followed by her older brother
Christopher Price
Has returned . . .

A huge golden hand
Pulls my dreams into the box . . .
Bang!
The desires have gone home.

Liam Sefton (11)
Ysgol Cynlais, Swansea

Scared

Scared is brown.
It tastes like damp sand,
It smells like earwax,
It looks like a nightmare,
It sounds like a bang in the night,
It feels like a hot kettle.
Scared is horrible.

Luke Price (10)
Ysgol Cynlais, Swansea

Excited

Excited is green.
It tastes like sugar cubes,
It smells like the bright breeze in your face,
It looks like Gavin Henson kicking
The winning penalty against England,
It sounds like the atmosphere of the new Ospreys Stadium,
It feels like the smooth pages in a wonderful book.
Excited is brilliant.

Tyla Phillips (9)
Ysgol Cynlais, Swansea

Love

Love is red.
It tastes like strawberry ice cream,
It smells like fresh flowers in a spring garden,
It looks like a big red heart,
It sounds like a fantastic song,
It feels like a smooth piece of paper.
It makes me feel happy!

Emma Broad (9)
Ysgol Cynlais, Swansea

Fear

Fear is grey.
It tastes like fruit from the tree of knowledge in the Bible,
It smells like rotten eggs
And looks like the end of the world.
It sounds like zombies groaning,
It looks like green slime.
Fear is haunting!

Adam Carpenter (9)
Ysgol Cynlais, Swansea

Happiness

Happiness is red.
It tastes like sweets,
It smells like new flowers,
It looks like a hot sun,
It sounds like a bird singing,
It feels like a comfy bed.
Happiness is lovely.

Gavin Jones (10)
Ysgol Cynlais, Swansea

Anger

Anger is black.
It tastes like hot chilli peppers,
It smells like choking black smoke,
It looks like a hot fire,
It sounds like a roaring dragon,
It feels like an ice cube.
Anger is horrible.

Katy Edwards (9)
Ysgol Cynlais, Swansea

Revenge

Revenge is dark red.
It tastes like blood from a body,
It smells of bad breath,
It looks like the army fighting,
It sounds like a gun firing,
It feels like holding a dead body in a coffin.
Revenge is horrible.

Connor Goodwin (9)
Ysgol Cynlais, Swansea

Anger

Anger is red.
It tastes like hot chilli peppers,
It smells like choking black smoke,
It looks like volcanic lava,
It sounds like a roaring dragon,
It feels like rough sandpaper.
Anger is evil.

Stephen Ellerby (9)
Ysgol Cynlais, Swansea

Love

Love is pink.
It tastes like candy sweets,
It smells like flowers growing in the garden,
It looks like a heart,
It sounds like laughter of children,
It feels like a furry pillow.
Love is beautiful.

Jessica Connick (9)
Ysgol Cynlais, Swansea

Happiness

Happiness is blue.
It tastes like a Twix,
It smells like chocolate,
It looks like a water park,
It sounds like a hippy song,
It feels like a comfortable warm bed.
Happiness is brilliant.

Martyn Davies (10)
Ysgol Cynlais, Swansea

Love

Love is pink.
It tastes like juicy strawberries,
It smells like perfume,
It looks like pretty red and pink roses,
It sounds like the birds singing in the morning,
It feels like the softness of silk.
Love is being happy.

Molly Carr (9)
Ysgol Cynlais, Swansea

Emotion

Happiness is like a red heart.
　　I place it in the dazzling blue sky,
Where it glows like a star.
　　I feed it with my love,
It changes into a passionate dove
　　And drifts away.

Claire Williams (11)
Ystruth School, Abertillery

Emotion

Bravery is a blue diamond,
I place it in an enchanted forest.
It glows all day.
I feed it with red roses.
It changes into a golden lion
And *roars*.

Shelley Heath (11)
Ystruth School, Abertillery

Emotion

Delight is a pink diamond,
I put it in the deep green forest.
It bursts out with song.
I feed it with love.
It changes into a gleaming butterfly
And flutters away.

Megan Heath (11)
Ystruth School, Abertillery

Emotion

Delight is a yellow circle.
I put it in the beautiful green field,
Where it spins around and around.
I feed it with happiness.
It changes into a blue and green butterfly
And it flies away.

Lauren Heath (11)
Ystruth School, Abertillery

Emotion

Violence is a black-thorned rose.
I put it in the jungle,
Where it spread violence around.
I feed it with animals' violence.
It changes into a venomous snake
And slithers away.

Ellen Wayman (11)
Ystruth School, Abertillery

Emotion

Loneliness is a blue square.
I put it in the sea.
It sits alone.
I feed it sunflower seeds.
It turns into a dolphin
And wave-hops away.

Kristi Reed (11)
Ystruth School, Abertillery

Emotion

Peace is a pink crystal.
I place it in a shimmering green field
Where it glistens all day.
I feed it with grass off the fields.
It changes into a dazzling unicorn
And it gallops away.

Sophie Mason (11)
Ystruth School, Abertillery

Emotion

Enchantment is a silver star.
I put it in the countryside.
It makes the flowers grow.
I feed it with my happiness.
It changes into a beautiful rose and disappears slowly.

Shannon Jones (11)
Ystruth School, Abertillery

Emotion

Peace is a blue crystal.
I place it in a waterfall.
It makes the water glisten.
I feed it with rose petals.
It turns into a sea horse
And it gallops away.

Megan Jones (11)
Ystruth School, Abertillery

Emotion

Joy is a silver diamond
I place it in a sparkling field
Where it makes the field smile.
I feed it with pride.
It changes into a dazzling dog
And sprints away.

Tori Williams (11)
Ystruth School, Abertillery

Emotion

Delight is a yellow square.
I place it into my drawer
Where it glows all day.
I feed it blue paper.
It changes into a shimmering hamster
And hops away.

Tomas Price (11)
Ystruth School, Abertillery

Emotion

Peace is a gold star.
I place it on a plant.
It sleeps all day.
I feed it with love.
It changes into a white dove that drifts away.

Mason Smith (11)
Ystruth School, Abertillery

Emotion

Contentment is a light blue sphere.
I place it in a lush green meadow.
It sends out beams of light to make
The meadow calm and peaceful.
I feed it with my sorrow.
It changes into a magnificent dove
And soars peacefully away
To create another green meadow.

Frances May (11)
Ystruth School, Abertillery

Emotion

Peace is an aqua rose.
I place it in a meadow.
It looks at all the views.
I feed it with my love and sorrow.
It changes to a horse
And gallops away into the night.

Abbie Hopkins (11)
Ystruth School, Abertillery

Emotion

Violence is a black diamond.
I place it in the thick green jungle.
It hunts faster than anything.
I feed it with my anger.
It changes into a black panther
And it moves unseen.

Steven Phillips (11)
Ystruth School, Abertillery